COPYRIGHT

PUBLISHED BY 7SEVEN SPARK PUBLISHING

WWW.LESLEYNURSE.COM | WWW.7SEVENSPARKPUBLISHING.COM

ISBN 979-8-218-25244-1

PRINTED IN THE UNITED STATES OF AMERICA

COVER DESIGN AND LAYOUT BY LESLEY D. NURSE

EDITED BY 7SEVEN SPARK PUBLISHING

CONTENTS

YOU'RE RIGHT I DON'T CARE

INTRODUCTION

You're right. I don't care is not just a catchy phrase or defense mechanism. It is about how to overcome taking things personally, worrying, and letting go of control of things that are out of our control. It is about breaking down the common triggers that get most of us in this stuck place that brings out anxiety, depression, fear, anger, and more.

**WE CAN'T EXPECT TO GET PAST THINGS
COMPLETELY
YET ALWAYS FIND OUR WAY BACK TO OUR SAFE
SPACE
. -Lesley**

Whether we like it or not, it, a.k.a fear, or whatever word that resonates better with you, has held more power than most of us care or want to admit. I had a moment of reflection and decided that I was ready to get past my wall.

At that moment, I knew that I had to be willing to do the most uncomfortable things to get to the other side of greatness. It would take me having the courage to speak my innermost truth and find true happiness in my life - on my own.

Why I wrote this book

My truth is that I have experienced emotional, verbal, and physical abuse starting at age thirteen. It's not something I ever wanted to share, but I thought that in this climate, to help other people, you had to know that I am also a survivor.

EVEN THOUGH SOME ABUSE STOPPED AT A YOUNGER AGE, IT CARRIED OVER TO MY ADULT YEARS IN MANY WAYS.

I struggled to understand how life could strike me twice like lightning, but then I had to accept that something bigger than me needed my help.

There was one thing.

I was not too fond of the thought of being seen as a victim. I grew up in an environment where everyone was tough and independent and took no mess from anyone. Although we struggled financially and lived in a one-bedroom apartment, you would never know it by the way we took pride in making it into something special.

I never knew we were making it on one income because, growing up; my mom didn't make me feel financially inferior. We dressed snazzy and were jazzy, but looking back, we had stuff, but what I desperately needed was comfort to express love and pain.

It was never the right time to voice my abuse. Mentally, I was not ready to adjust to my ordeal. I denied it and hid it for as long as I could. It's like I was two different people. I wanted to make my fatherless family proud, and I tried to fix my problems independently as a teenager. Is anyone else guilty?

There was something that haunted me for years. I felt like I didn't do enough to protect myself, and I spent years trying to get it from other people and being protective of myself. I felt that because I knew that I survived, God would give me a pass at some point. Certain friends would make up for others who let me down. Someone would love me the way that I never got from an absentee father, and boy, did I have to start from scratch and relearn everything in a nontoxic way.

IT WAS HARD, BUT I WAS MOTIVATED TO CHANGE THE PATH THAT I WAS HEADING

I was beginning a new journey of self-discovery. During this phase, dominance from music to the culture was vital. No one knew that in our world, it was possible to improve our lives. As hard-working immigrants of the West Indies, if it didn't first involve making money, it just didn't make any sense.

Even though we went through some dark times, I knew that I had a little voice inside that started whispering to me, and I had a new friend called Spirit. Fast forward to today; everything that I do now involves my new friend, helping to inspire others.

Growing up, I never connected with one public figure and needed help that wasn't there. Relationships became the way that I learned what worked and didn't.

Until I found there was a little light in me. There was power in me, and I had choices I never considered. I could be who I wanted to be and not explode because I didn't address the issues that I didn't know were issues. It was a mess, and so was I.

That's why I had to write this book. What if another Lesley out there needs this? They could be hiding in plain sight, and no one knows, or they don't know how to seek help. What if there is someone who wants to learn where they went wrong?

I chose the number 7 as it holds significant spiritual value, and it is a number I incorporate into my products and brands to convey inspirational messages. The book I have created is designed to be easily digestible, allowing you to finish it during your commute while traveling, or while unwinding on a beach.

Wherever you are, I hope these lessons I learned help you find a way like it was able to help me. You might be at a place you don't like, but at the end of this book, I hope you will feel more confident and equipped to get where you want to be.

Happy reading.

Xoxo,

LESSON

1

SWITCHING UP YOUR ACTIONS WILL HELP SWITCH "INTO" NEW RESULTS.

I got tired of repeating the same cycles. Through that time being in the " woods" myself, people viewed this as a badge of courage to keep a fit of fiery anger going while growing up. If I got frustrated by someone not keeping their word or missing the mark, I would always keep a massive grudge or lash out. While in the woods, I held in pain and endured a lot of pain, and I just couldn't let it go. By doing this, I would heal, then hurt, then hurt and heal, while never doing anything new to improve.

This is not about blaming the past. This is about being tired and motivated enough to want to improve your life now. No matter what your background is, things can improve, but it takes work.

WHAT WORK, MIGHT YOU ASK?

It's not like a workout in a gym or working at a job that you hate. Well, it could feel like that at times. Now that I'm thinking more about it. It feels like working only to pay bills but then being happy when the benefits kick in! It might feel unfair and take longer than you would prefer, but you won't know until you start.

Think about it. When you're used to handling things a certain way all of your life or have little knowledge of how to handle a specific issue, there will be a learning curve. Change takes dedication to overcome, repeating the same patterns. You can start today by making small adjustments that will have significant effects.

HERE ARE SOME QUICK TIPS THAT CAN HELP YOU STOP REPEATING THE SAME HABITS.

Tips

HERE ARE SOME QUICK TIPS THAT CAN HELP YOU STOP REPEATING THE SAME HABITS

TIP 1: CREATE AFFIRMATIONS

You can start by looking in the mirror and saying in the mirror that ***I am new and ready, that is old and unsteady***. Try it! You can say something else if you prefer. It has to be extreme in action, catchy enough to remember, and powerful enough to serve the purpose of helping to stop practicing your habits now. While you can't control how others will react, you can hold yourself accountable and stick to breaking the pattern.

TIP 2: CREATE A LANGUAGE SUPERPOWER

Pick any other language that you don't know, pick a tune that works best for you, and apply it to your triggers. It will feel weird at first, but it will get better. Start to playback those sounds when you hear, talk about self-doubt, or when someone is irritating you. You will see a change in no time.

TIP 3: WRITE IT AND REPEAT IT

You can try writing new habits. You can write what you will do and no longer do and repeat it over and over again. For example, You can also write that you will handle all criticism well. If you tend to be defensive, you can write that you will no longer be defensive. The goal is not to be tricky or aim for perfection; it's to break the cycle and get new and improved results. You got this!

TIP 4: DON'T SAVE USING LOVE FOR JUST GOOD TIMES BUT USE IT BRAVELY FOR THE NEGATIVE SITUATIONS TOO

There is a saying that misery loves company. Pain is real, and pain loves to get you to react! It doesn't matter if you have the best comeback reply, facts, or a well-received person. The point is to refrain from engaging. By letting love lead, you redirect a new shift in your life with higher results. Plus, you will leave them speechless!

Have fun!

I Choose To...

Take your time and share your future plans or aspirations after completing this chapter. Remember, there are no right or wrong answers.

A	C	T	R	A	M	S
W	M	P	Y	O	L	T
E	P	A	X	D	O	R
S	U	R	Z	N	V	O
O	Y	Q	Y	I	I	N
M	N	I	I	K	N	G
E	N	K	Q	N	G	G
X	U	S	A	W	U	O
R	F	E	H	C	F	C
E	Y	T	T	E	R	P

FIND 9 WORDS ABOUT
YOU

I Choose To...

I Choose To...

I Choose To...

LESSON

DO EMOTIONAL FASTINGS

There will be times when you have to take a break from the world. It's so easy to go day to day like clockwork. We practice habits that sometimes are oblivious to ourselves. We take the same route to work. We eat the same breakfast. We drink the same cocktails. We wear the same colors.

What about reacting the same emotionally?

For me, I found that no matter what the situation was, my reactions were the same most of the time. If it upset me, it pained me for three days. If I was sad, it lasted for three days.

IT WASN'T UNTIL I GAVE MYSELF PERMISSION AND SAW THAT I WAS ON A TIMER THAT I REALIZED THAT I WANTED DIFFERENT RESULTS.

I'm not too fond of patterns, either. But here I was, living by a design that I created based on my thoughts and emotions. I wondered, when I was upset, how come other people were still smiling? Didn't they know that today was a sad day? Or so I thought. It got horrible, and I hated how I felt and how heavy my mind was, and I decided that I wanted to smile and get over it.

IT TOOK PRACTICE, BUT I STARTED MY NEW FASTING REGIMEN BY FASTING EMOTIONALLY AND MENTALLY.

I created a time limit with emotions. By creating this lifestyle move, I freed up turning worry into depression, anger, and resentment and avoided making rash decisions based on temporary feelings and thoughts. It doesn't have to be a negative situation, either.

It could be event planning or shopping for the perfect gift. The point is to give yourself time to think about it and come up with solutions, then move on. If you stay in the same place with no way out, you'll keep going around and around in circles only to end back up where you started.

Tips

TIP 1: ASSESS THE SITUATION

You can start by assessing the situation head-on. Ask yourself, is this thought or problem feeding me or starving me? Is it motivating me to grow, be inspired, or help someone in need? Or is it draining me, making me feel stuck, restricted, and uninspired to move forward?

Don't get me wrong; sometimes, you have to be a shoulder for others. If you are a leader, you are asked for more and often given less in return. However, when you give and give and give, your mental, emotional, and spiritual health needs to know when enough is enough.

TIP 2: SET A MENTAL TIMER

The following action is what I like to describe as a mental timer. It is effortless to fall into depression and worry, and one way to snap out of it or keep it moving is to

end the dark energy and ask yourself if this is feeding you, meaning, is this making you happy or peaceful? Or, it is depriving you, meaning zapping your energy and disturbing your peace. Tend to your mental and emotional needs and then move forward.

TIP 3: COME UP WITH SOLUTIONS

It's easy to have strong feelings or worry about something. But you have to push forward, taking action steps. This might sound like a no-brainer, but it's often mowed over by emotions or endless thoughts of the same issues. You can retrain yourself to snap out of your "woods" by changing the patterns and creating a new one.

TIP 4: SET LIMITS

This is for the ones who want to grow. How do you know if you want it? By setting boundaries. Say no, be less available if it conflicts with your me-time. Give other people's problems attention without it reaching the level of exhausting your own joy. Reserve time for yourself and reflect, relax, and release. This is a selfish act but a vital one if you want to be the best version of yourself. If you are the best version of yourself, only then will you be able to do so before you can show up for others.

Have fun!

Take your time and share your future plans or aspirations after completing this chapter. Remember, there are no right or wrong answers.

_____
_____
_____
_____
_____
_____
_____
_____
_____
_____
_____
_____
_____
_____
_____
_____
_____
_____
_____
_____
_____
_____
_____
_____
_____
_____

I Choose To...

I Choose To...

I Choose To...

P	C	A	L	M	B	T
L	E	E	T	W	N	N
E	P	A	X	Q	I	E
A	L	R	C	B	A	D
S	J	O	Y	E	T	I
U	M	I	P	K	R	F
R	U	K	P	M	E	N
E	A	S	A	W	C	O
R	E	E	H	C	F	C
E	P	T	S	U	R	T

FIND 9 WORDS ABOUT
JOY

LESSON

YOU CAN'T DO THE SELF-WORK FOR OTHER PEOPLE

We all have things to work on and, from time to time, need someone to lean on too. However, when it comes to it being a routine, and you are trying to do things for other people so they can learn instead of letting them know to do it for themselves, that is called enabling.

I GET IT. SOME PEOPLE NEED HELP. IT COULD BE FINANCIAL, EMOTIONAL, OR PHYSICAL.

It gets dicey when the first thing that you do is offer to do it for them. They don't have to worry a lot. They don't have to feel pain for too long or feel lost or have to step up.

And that can cause resentment, ungratefulness, and immaturity in return. Instead of what you really hoped for, which is self-awareness, appreciation, and growth.

SHOULDN'T WE BE THERE FOR OTHER PEOPLE THAT WE CARE ABOUT?

Yes and no. Yes, you should be there and support others in a way that you can afford to help but also do it with love, transparency, and fairness to your heart. No, it wouldn't be best to be there for them if you were crossed one too many times.

For example, if you lend money to someone with a track record of not paying you back because something happened again. I understand that you don't want to see them suffer or lose their valuable possessions. But if they have a habit of abusing your kindness, how kind are you really being to you?

JUMPING IN THE MIDDLE OF THEIR DRAMAS

I got so used to being tolerant of pain and emotional baggage that when someone gave it to me, I volunteered with no second thoughts.

But, allowing them to dump their emotional baggage or dilemmas on me only left me broken, and unappreciated. This didn't motivate anyone to change. Enabling them only kept this going strong like a cup of black coffee.

THIS IS NOT ABOUT BEING A VICTIM OF ABUSE OR BLAMING OTHER PEOPLE.

This is about establishing clear lines of communication and expectations. But this goes both ways, for every action is a reaction. And we can only seek change if we are ready and willing to change first.

Let's face it; at times, it's not mutual, and rather than turn it into a competition or resentment party, it's time to redesign how you can show up for other people without being responsible for them.

Tips

HERE ARE SOME QUICK TIPS THAT CAN HELP YOU STOP
REPEATING THE SAME HABITS

TIP 1: PULL BACK

Pull back and look closely at what you do routinely to help assist in a situation. Do you get too involved emotionally? Do you give too much of your opinion and need more listening? This is not to pick apart your kind gesture; however, it is necessary to see where there is a need for a balance between support and taking care of the situation.

TIP 2: SELF REFLECT

Is this about them or about you? What motivates you to take on their problems and energy at this level of intensity? Is it a case of unresolved issues from your past that you wish someone did something different for you?

Or is it an ego boost? Answering these questions honestly identifies your motives and the best method to help you adjust your habits of taking on more load than you should.

TIP 3: ENCOURAGE THEM WITH WORDS AND LEAD BY EXAMPLE

If you're concerned about sounding preachy or judgy, you can show support by leading by example and encouraging them. Show a better way through your actions and be consistent. Also, feel free to give back positive reinforcement anytime you see the effort. It doesn't have to be overkill for more than it really is. Just offering a " good job" will suffice. When specific feedback is given, it can motivate change, and they are more than likely to appreciate the support and be inspired to do more.

TIP 4: LEAVE IT ALONE

By this time. One of two things is happening. They are falling and getting back up, or they are resisting change and resentful of your growth. Either way, you now have more energy and space to be a better you, and everyone can respect that.

I Choose To...

Take your time and share your future plans or aspirations after completing this chapter. Remember, there are no right or wrong answers.

_____
_____
_____
_____
_____
_____
_____
_____
_____
_____
_____
_____
_____
_____
_____
_____
_____
_____
_____
_____
_____
_____
_____

I Choose To...

I Choose To...

I Choose To...

LESSON

PROTECT YOUR PEACE AT ALL COSTS

By this point, I hope that you've gained more clarity. The lessons I have learned are all collectively part of a new foundation after I tore down my old ways. Like so many of us, while growing up, I was raised upholding other people's thinking and habits of what they learned and how they handled things.

BUT THEN I HAD TO LEARN MY WAY.

This brings me to why protecting my peace is so critical. It might seem like it's enough to stop being an enabler or practicing emotional fasting, and life will be better. I say, not so fast.

After you start to have a more straightforward path, it's time to build up your protective shield. Nothing comes in, and nothing goes out.

We hear about protective styles and protection for our skin when we're out basking in the sun. What about protection for our spirit and mind? I can't tell you how crucial this step is to worry less. As much as I would like to say that once you practice these new habits, it will always be unicorns and rainbow sprinkles. It gets deeper.

THE TRUTH IS, YOU WILL AGGRAVATE SOME PEOPLE TO THE POINT OF MAKING THEM VERY ANNOYED WITH YOUR MATURITY

They can't understand how you can smile when your life has problems, struggle to pay your bills or find the right relationship. Why do you seem unbreakable? Why? Because you learned why it's essential to protect your heart with your light.

AND I'M GOING TO SHOW YOU HOW....

Tips

HERE ARE SOME QUICK TIPS THAT CAN HELP YOU STOP
REPEATING THE SAME HABITS

TIP 1: RAISE THE BAR FROM WITHIN

You have accepted the low, tired, nasty, and confusing treatment for way too long. Now it's time to raise the bar by elevating yourself. It doesn't mean that you change your personality. It's about cherishing and putting the magnetic light that shines within you to work. Once you activate it and let it know what is acceptable and no longer acceptable, it goes to town on your behalf.

TIP 2: PRACTICE A NEW SELF-TALK

Habits are formed by repeating them daily, so it takes new habits to undo what was previously in effect. Sometimes, your mind will play tricks on you and make you second-guess your new patterns.

That is where self-talk comes in. Talkback! Remember to keep it kind and straightforward; after all, you are retraining your self-consciousness to think and react differently now. Be consistent and patient with your progress.

TIP 3: BE PREPARED FOR TESTS

Mountains of tests of your determination will surely come. This is new territory. You can armor your unique self with simple changes by setting up your safe space. You can do little things like listening to uplifting music and audiobooks or speaking to the most supportive people in your life.

Get in the habit of complimenting yourself and claiming to have a great day, no matter what. Treat yourself to a Mani and Pedi and look your best. You'd be surprised by taking care of yourself, and making small changes can change many things.

TIP 4: GET YOUR PRIORITIES IN ORDER

For those who need to get more established with their finances or relationships that no longer feed you, then this is the step to take.

Part of protecting your heart with your inner light is also doing a clean sweep of what no longer suits you. Once you do that, it is a light party.

WOW, WE ARE GETTING THRU THESE LESSONS. WE HAVE THREE CRUCIAL LESSONS LEFT THAT I LEARNED TO CARE LESS. WE ARE ALMOST THERE.

LET'S GO!

Have fun!

I Choose To...

Take your time and share your future plans or aspirations after completing this chapter. Remember, there are no right or wrong answers.

_____
_____
_____
_____
_____
_____
_____
_____
_____
_____
_____
_____
_____
_____
_____
_____
_____
_____
_____
_____
_____
_____
_____
_____
_____

I Choose To...

I Choose To...

I Choose To...

LESSON

DON'T TAKE TO HEART WHAT THEY THINK OR DO

When other people's opinions and energy seep into your mind, it can do real damage if you are not careful. Everyone has opinions and experiences in life. However, it's easy for others to see you how they see themselves. That can be a good thing or a terrible thing. Either way, they both stifle and cloud your self-perception, and that's a no-no for your personal growth.

WORDS HAVE POWER

And it's necessary not to let it have control over the way that you see yourself. Don't get me wrong; this is not a pass to deflect your actions at times. It is about your ability to not waiver about your value and worth when the world says something that you might not want to hear or deserve.

YOU HAVE HIGHER POWER THAN WORDS.

Words can have a lasting impact on the way that you see yourself. It doesn't matter how prideful or sensitive you might be. All it takes are some stinging words to damage our self-worth for years or the rest of our lives. You might get tempted to fight back against obstacles that may come your way - but eventually, you will get tired.

I know because I got tired too. I got tired of fussing and having to win the last word. Frankly, I just kept missing the mark with my reactions. The most significant healing factor was honing my ability to separate my value from other people's views. Changing habits is not a one-day decision. It is a lifestyle. Here are some tips you can start today to see a vast difference in your life now!

Tips

HERE ARE SOME QUICK TIPS THAT CAN HELP YOU STOP REPEATING THE SAME HABITS

TIP 1: PRACTICE FORGIVENESS

Practicing forgiving will make a happier living. Forgiving might seem like the last thing you would think of doing when trying to avoid taking other views or actions to heart. I used to think that way until I learned that not letting things go only piled on more of the same situations along the way.

When you forgive yourself and let go of the angst and thoughts, you free up your mind and energy to move forward and start a new clean slate. When you forgive others, you decide to move forward instead of repeating the same scenario; this gets you quicker to the best part of yourself.

TIP 2: COME UP WITH OTHER SOLUTIONS

We all have been there. We argue with someone close or distant and have our weaponry to prove our points. We get upset, even cry, leading us to say or do things we don't mean. It just got to the point that handling things that way no longer suited me.

I WANTED TO CUT OUT THE FAT OF EMOTIONS

Imagine cutting out the fat and getting to solutions. What if you had the talk by yourself and imagined what the other person would a person say? Have you considered their side? Do you have to be, right? Detach your wants and needs and think win-win.

If it's more important to win, then there will be no room to lose to ego or outdated thoughts and get to a new and improved way of thinking. If it's more important to grow, then let's get to the next tip that worked for me.

TIP 3: LAUGH IT OFF

No rule says you can't laugh at things that bother you or linger in your mind. This step runs deeper because you subconsciously are re-shifting how you received the information. This is a power move. Think of it as changing the temperature on the thermostat, and we are playing it oh so cool.

TIP 4: ADJUST WHERE NEEDED

If others widely share feedback about you, then it's worth exploring for more truth. Finding the truth is a good thing, and don't be afraid or too prideful to adjust. The universe is nudging us to shift sometimes, and we do everything to say it isn't so. Sometimes seeing it as a clue is more accessible than a critique. By looking at it from an accepting place, adjusting will be intriguing instead of feeling forced to make a change.

Have fun!

I Choose To...

Take your time and share your
future plans or aspirations after
completing this chapter.
Remember, there are no right or
wrong answers.

_____
_____
_____
_____
_____
_____
_____
_____
_____
_____
_____
_____
_____
_____
_____
_____
_____
_____
_____
_____
_____
_____
_____
_____

I Choose To...

I Choose To...

I Choose To...

_____
_____
_____
_____
_____
_____
_____
_____
_____
_____
_____
_____
_____
_____
_____
_____
_____
_____
_____
_____
_____
_____
_____
_____
_____
_____
_____
_____
_____

LESSON #

STOP SAYING YES WHEN IT'S REALLY NO

I am neither a party person nor like to wait in long lines. I love finding ways to reduce wasted time and get things done. For me, this makes me happy. But for others, this could be seen as boring, antisocial, or only interested in one's likes. Maybe maybe not.

QUIETNESS BRINGS ME JOY, BUT IT MIGHT DRIVE SOMEONE ELSE CRAZY.

What honors your joy? It's about more than just attending events. It's really about saying yes to what feeds you peace. Trying to live up to their or your ctations will only leave someone trapped by guilt.

Believe it or not, saying no to things that you don't want to do or agree with will free you up to live your life more authentically. Why put that kind of pressure on others or yourself? While you're being fearful of disappointing them, they could be thinking something completely different. Learn to say no; when it is a no, instead of saying yes to please other people, show care for your soul.

LESLEY, YOU DON'T KNOW MY LIFE; I JUST CAN'T SAY NO

I ask why. What are the alternatives to facing your fears? Most fears come from perceptions based on one's life experiences. So many people think that sweeping things under the rug or self-medicating or overworking will be helpful. In the short term, I can see why that would be a smart choice, but in the long run, these methods are only going to do more damage than good.

YOUR HEALTH NEEDS THE BEST YOU

I'm a firm believer that what you think and how you think affects your health. Have you ever felt tense in the neck or shoulders or had bad headaches? I'm sure there are more parts of the body, but these stand out for me. When the aches ring, you have to answer the call.

Tips

HERE ARE SOME QUICK TIPS THAT CAN HELP YOU STOP
REPEATING THE SAME HABITS

TIP 1: SAY NO

Saying no might seem like a no-brainer, but often, we dance around speaking our true feelings to avoid saying the wrong thing. Or, we'll delay giving a reply when in all actuality, the answer is no.

Why wait until the last minute or say you forgot when you know your answer? Most people will understand that if you come from a kind place with your truth and respond in a respectable time frame, you would be okay if the tables were turned towards you. If saying no hurts too much, use emojis if necessary. Say no if it's a no.

TIP 2: WRITE NO

If you don't feel right saying no, then write it. If the person emailed you, then you can respond the same way. Or, if they didn't, and you feel more shy or reserved, you can start the conversation with an email. This method depends on the relationship. If you're going to communicate effectively, with a close friend, for example, another conversation should take place.

TIP 3: CALL THE PERSON

If writing doesn't work for you, then you might feel more confident speaking on the phone. When someone texts or emails, they show no tone. And these methods leave us to interpret the delivery from our perspective. At least by speaking over the phone, there is an opportunity to clear up any misconceptions, give more details and make room for new plans.

TIP 4: COMBINE THE METHODS
Sometimes, a short and sweet no will suffice as well.

It's important to keep the people you care about informed about your plans. However, you don't have to feel obliged to update them constantly. Just touch base with them quickly and then make your decision. You don't want to encourage any clinginess or demands from others.
Keep your communication balanced.

ave
fun!

I Choose To...

Take your time and share your
future plans or aspirations after
completing this chapter. Remember,
here are no right or wrong answers.

I Choose To...

I Choose To...

I Choose To...

LESSON

OWN WHAT MAKES YOU UNIQUELY YOU

Being transparent with my struggles shows you that you're not alone and it can get better. You can live a life free of worry, but it takes great discipline and re-shifting your feelings. The only difference is knowing how to manage them better. There's so much more about you that you are yet to discover.

YOU AND I GET TO CREATE IT, BE IT, AND OWN IT.

No more apologizing for what makes other people or yourself uncomfortable.

Because the truth is, as long as you live authentically unapologetically, there will be discomfort in some shape or form that will come. It's part of the change, and that's okay.

THE BIGGER PICTURE IS, SO WHAT, BE YOU ANYWAY!

Be you with your personality, style, looks, laugh, pain, healing, and who you are on your way to becoming. Own how you love and whom you love and, most importantly, what makes you uniquely you. Being yourself, you never should apologize or downplay who you are! That's the beauty of what makes you uniquely you.

There is no perfect person because perfection is in our minds. Even though it might seem there is a standard of perfection, it is what you agree to, not what other people tell you that it is.

CARING LESS IS ABOUT LIVING MORE BY YOUR ESSENTIALS OF HAPPINESS.

Take it with you everywhere and never leave home without it again. As you get better, you will start to see the negative feelings less and less and go away much quicker.

There will be times when you face obstacles in life, and you need time to process them. We all do. The key is to stay there only a short time and move forward to finding solutions.

SO I INVITE YOU TO THROW CARE TO THE WIND AS I HAVE AND LIVE MORE FOR YOU!

By caring less and doing what's best for you, you can make time to touch up internal matters, such as listening more to your inner self. Using this concept will allow you to return to the world happier, healthier, and more present than ever. When you make this shift, the world will shift along with you.

You are loved and have so much more inside you waiting for your signal to shine! Reward yourself with more time and attention that you need. Listen to your quiet voice and body when it speaks through strains of pain.

IF YOU DON'T TAKE A LEAP OF FAITH IN YOURSELF FIRST, WHO WILL?

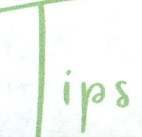

D	L	I	U	B	E	R
L	E	E	R	E	N	I
E	P	A	E	N	I	S
R	R	U	C	D	A	E
O	J	O	O	U	T	I
T	E	I	V	K	R	F
S	E	K	E	M	D	E
E	R	S	R	W	N	O
R	F	I	X	C	E	C
E	V	O	R	P	M	I

FIND 9 WORDS ABOUT

HEALING

Have fun!

I Choose To...

Take your time and share your future plans or aspirations after completing this chapter. Remember, there are no right or wrong answers.

I Choose To...

I Choose To...

I Choose To...

If you have no balance or inner cheerleader to speak on your behalf, you will think it's impossible to see improvements. Blessings don't just come in shiny gift wrap; they also come in repeating cycles trying to get your attention.

It takes time; that's why I wanted to give you plenty of tips that worked for me that I still use to this day. It is not a phase, this is a lifestyle, and if you don't train your mind, it will run all over you. Now that you have read my lessons learned, it's time to put in the work in your life.

When you apply it, you won't ever have to struggle to live a more fulfilling life. Give it your dedication, time, and, most importantly, give yourself time.

Here's to you cleaning out the mess and making more time for the best version of you to shine through!

LESLEY D. NURSE

Break Free and Create Your Dream Life
Lesley is dedicated to empowering people to overcome
their limitations and reach their full potential. Her
authentic and wise words invite you to embark on a
transformative journey toward self-discovery and
personal growth. Let Lesley inspire you to unlock your
true potential.

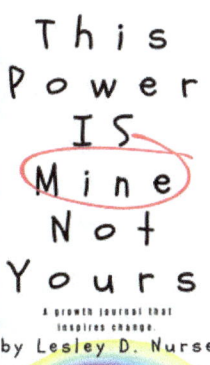  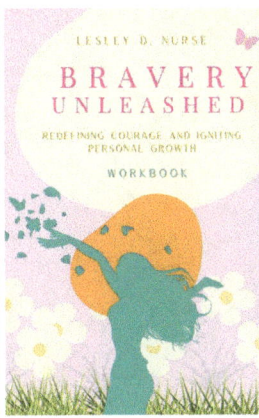 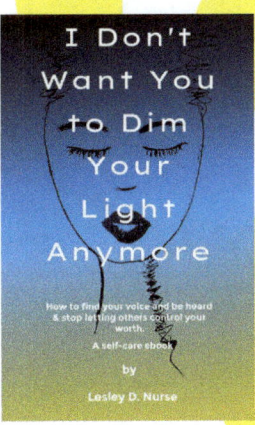

Discover Lesley's captivating collection of books and explore her diverse range of passions on her website. Her inspiring content will encourage you to embrace change, unlock your potential, and manifest the life you've always dreamed of. Lesley is dedicated to empowering you and will provide a trustworthy and engaging experience that will leave you feeling motivated and ready to conquer whatever challenges come your way.

WWW.LESLEYNURSE.COM

YOU'RE RIGHT. I DON'T CARE

In this section, you can describe scenarios that involve your thoughts, things that bother you or cause you distress, or keep you awake at night. After each entry, challenge yourself to come up with a solution to the problem. With practice, you will be surprised at the person you will become. You may even discover new things about yourself.